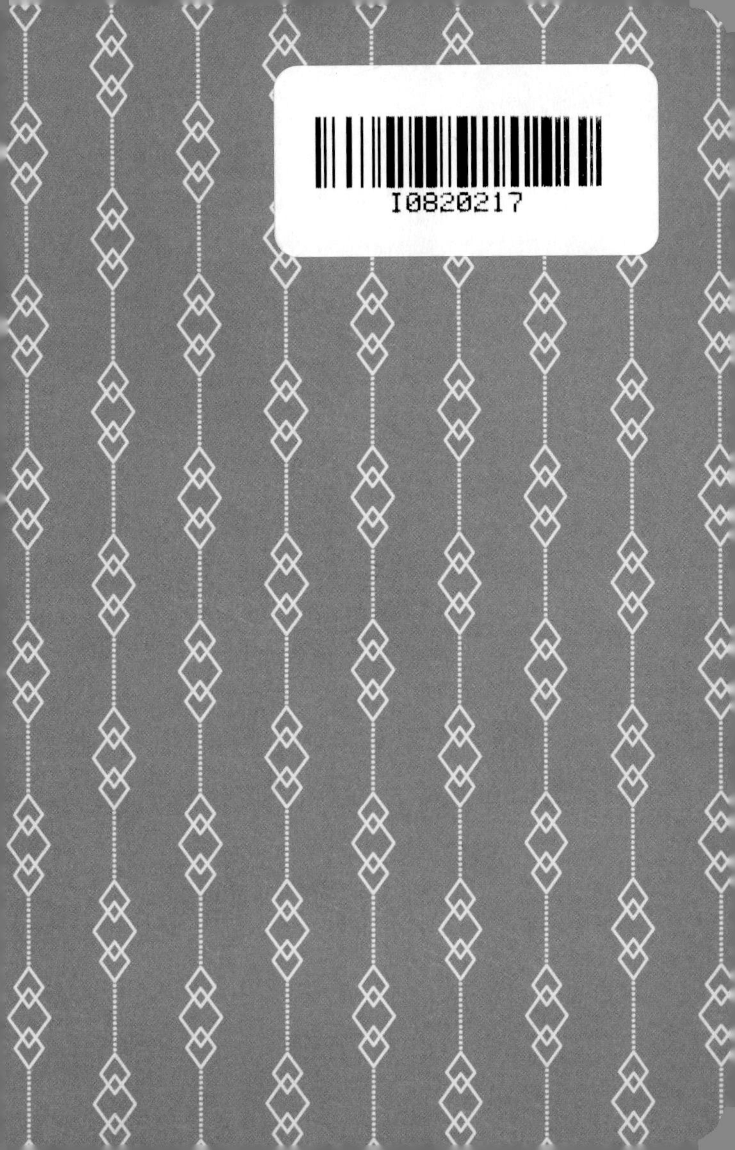
I0820217

POCKETBOOKS
by BroadStreet

100 Bible Promises

FOR MEN

BroadStreet
PUBLISHING

BroadStreet Publishing Group, LLC.
Savage, Minnesota, USA
Broadstreetpublishing.com

100 Bible Promises for Men

9781424571703
9781424571710 (eBook)

Devotional entries compiled and edited by Natasha Marcellus.

Typesetting and design by Garborg Design Works | garborgdesign.com
Editorial services by Michelle Winger | literallyprecise.com

Printed in China.

26 27 28 29 30 31 32 7 6 5 4 3 2 1

Introduction

Strong promises. Steadfast faith. Encouragement for every step.

Life brings challenges, pressures, and decisions that can feel overwhelming, but God's Word offers strength, clarity, and peace. This pocket-sized companion filled with powerful Scriptures, brief devotions, and heartfelt prayers will remind you of God's unshakable truth.

Whether you're facing a tough decision, seeking courage, or simply need encouragement, this book is a reminder that you are never alone, and God's promises are always enough. Keep it in your pocket, glovebox, or nightstand, and turn to it anytime you need strength, direction, or hope.

You are called, equipped, and never forsaken. Let God's promises lead you forward.

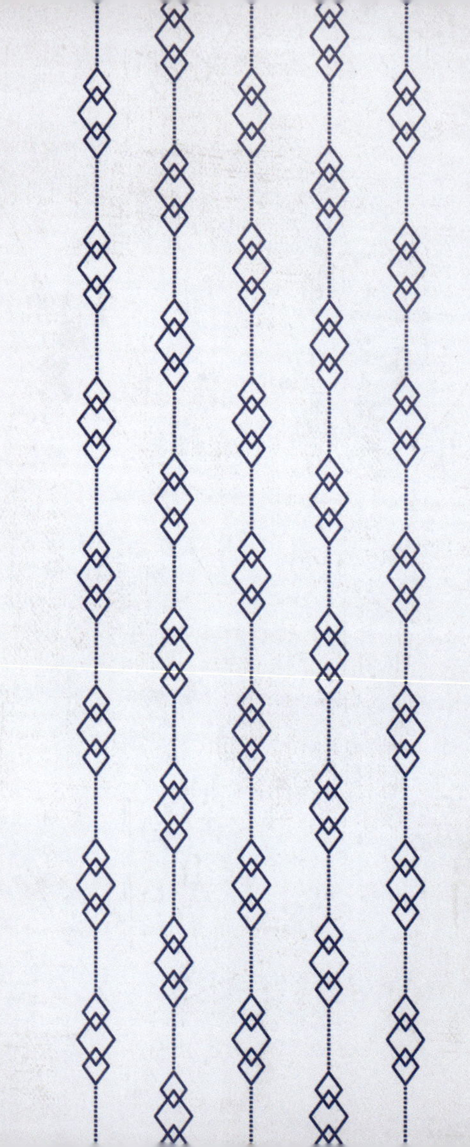

A Changed Life

This same Good News that came to you is going out all over the world. It is bearing fruit everywhere by changing lives, just as it changed your lives from the day you first heard and understood the truth about God's wonderful grace.

COLOSSIANS 1:6 NLT

The good news of Jesus is that our sins are forgiven and our relationship with God is restored through his saving work on the cross. This seed, when planted, grows and bears fruit for generations.

You have a remarkable twofold calling: embrace the good news wherever you are and share it with anyone you encounter. Sow the seeds of the gospel and help others cultivate their faith. Watch with joy as the good news spreads through them. Jesus has impacted your life so you can impact others.

God, let me never cover up my faith. Empower me to be bold in the way that I live out my commitment to you.

Fullness

I pray that you, being rooted and firmly established in love, may be able to comprehend with all the saints what is the length and width, height and depth of God's love, and to know Christ's love that surpasses knowledge, so that you may be filled with all the fullness of God.

EPHESIANS 3:17-19 CSB

Christ's love brings fullness of life. It was his love for humanity that pushed him to sacrifice so much on our behalf. It is through that same love that we are invited into a rich and satisfying life. His love is the missing puzzle piece for those who are yet to follow him.

The promise of Christ's love is that you have been made complete. Your own life is transformed, and you are able to live with more power and purpose than you ever could alone.

God, please continue pouring into me. Help me to experience your love in a way that fills my life.

Contentedness

I know what it is to be in need, and I know what it is to have plenty. I have learned the secret of being content in any and every situation, whether well fed or hungry, whether living in plenty or in want.

PHILIPPIANS 4:12 NIV

We often think that contentment comes with the fulfillment of all our needs and wants. If that were true, it would only be possible to be content when everything is perfect. God gives us the power and peace to be okay even when everything around us is not.

You don't have to chase a constantly moving target to find satisfaction. Scripture promises that contentment is possible, and God has given you everything you need to find it.

God, please give me your perspective. Help me to be content even when there are things I wish I could change. Help me to trust that you are always enough.

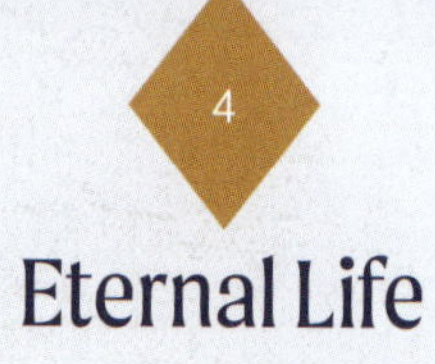

Eternal Life

"This is how God loved the world: He gave his one and only son, so that everyone who believes in him will not perish but have eternal life."

JOHN 3:16 NLT

Those of us who follow Jesus have been given the gift of eternal life. In exchange for our belief and devotion, we receive the indescribable joy of escaping death. We will live forever in the perfection of God's presence. He has created an eternal home for us, and our time on earth is temporary.

Your devotion to Christ guarantees you a place at God's table. You are an heir in his kingdom, and your status cannot be taken away from you. It is promised, and it is free.

Father, you loved me so much that you sent your Son to pay for my sin. He took my place, and I am forever grateful.

Identity

You are a chosen race, a royal priesthood, a holy nation, a people for his possession, so that you may proclaim the praises of the one who called you out of darkness into his marvelous light. Once you were not a people, but now you are God's people; you had not received mercy, but now you have received mercy.

1 Peter 2:9-10 CSB

Following Jesus comes with the promise of a new identity. It means adjusting our understanding of who we are. We are no longer defined by our own strengths or weaknesses, but we look to God for our sense of purpose and belonging. He created us, and he reassures us of our position in his kingdom.

God intentionally picked you. He didn't settle for you, and he didn't begrudgingly accept you; he chose you on purpose and for a purpose. You have been called into a role of great significance.

Father, thank you for choosing me. Thank you for accepting me instead of rejecting me. I am yours.

You can trust God with your heart and your life.

Help and Correction

All Scripture is God-breathed and is useful for teaching, rebuking, correcting and training in righteousness, so that the servant of God may be thoroughly equipped for every good work.

2 Timothy 3:16-17 NIV

Every word of Scripture holds weight and significance. The entire Bible is available to us whenever we need it. Our unhindered access to the Word is an incredible and profound gift. The pages of Scripture offer us help, guidance, encouragement, and correction through every season.

Don't take Scripture for granted. Write it on your heart and let it grow deep roots within you. Listen to it, memorize it, and take full advantage of its richness.

God, I want to know your Word so I can apply it when opportunities arise. Help me cling to your promises.

True Purpose

"Follow me, and I will make you fishers of men."

Matthew 4:19 NKJV

We tend to get lost in the idea of having a calling. We want to fulfill God's purposes for us, and we worry about doing it just the right way. The truth is that while the personal details might differ, we are each given the same set of instructions. God calls us to be fishers of men.

You don't have to go searching for your calling, and you don't have to wonder what you are supposed to do with your life. You are called to love people. Follow Christ's example and lay your life down for the people around you.

God, help me be a fisher of men. Thank you for giving me a purpose in your kingdom.

Safety in Numbers

Where there is no guidance, a people falls,
but in an abundance of counselors there is safety.

PROVERBS 11:14 ESV

There is safety in the counsel of others. We aren't meant to navigate life alone. We each have limited perspectives, and we are often blind to our faults. When we work together, we have the benefit of leaning on each other's strengths.

You cannot possibly handle every problem in your life alone. Scripture says that you are better off listening to the counsel of many people rather than simply trusting yourself. Safety is promised when you search for counsel.

God, thank you for the wisdom of others. Thank you for the promise of safety in counsel.

New Creation

If anyone is in Christ, he is a new creation; the old has passed away, and see, the new has come!

2 Corinthians 5:17 csb

The promise of the Christian life is not a better or improved life. The promise of following Jesus is a completely new life! The transforming power of God is so strong that it actively erases our old desires and ways of thinking. We are made new as we embrace God's character and purposes.

You are a new creation, having been made new simply by choosing to follow Jesus. You don't need to worry about your past any longer. Just keep following Jesus. Allow him to fill you with hope as you are transformed into his likeness.

God, thank you for making me new. I'm grateful that you did more than just polish me up or make me presentable; you completely re-created my way of living.

You have been called into a role of great significance.

Keep Going

As for you, brothers, do not grow weary in doing good.

2 Thessalonians 3:13 ESV

We all grow weary doing the right thing. We all get tired of laying our lives down for others. It's normal and perfectly human to feel the weight of self-sacrifice. This is why Scripture urges us to persevere. God knows that we struggle and are tempted to quit.

Keep going. Don't grow weary now. It's possible you won't see the results of your devotion, but nothing you give to God is fruitless. He will fulfill all of his promises, and he promises to reward those who stay faithful.

God, strengthen me to keep living how you ask me to live. Give me the endurance to make the decisions that please you.

Protected

The Lord is faithful, and he will strengthen you and protect you from the evil one.

2 Thessalonians 3:3 NIV

If we try to keep up with world events, we will quickly realize that the outlook seems grim. We are surrounded by turmoil, evil, and despair. Suffering is rampant, and it can be easy to get caught up in negativity.

God promises you protection from the evil one. He offers you his strength and covering. He is your refuge in times of trouble, and you can rely on him when it seems like everything is falling apart. If you are surrendered to him, he will keep you safe.

God, lift me up when I am overcome by the suffering I see. I trust you to strengthen me when I need it most.

Stronghold

The Lord is good,
a stronghold in a day of distress;
he cares for those who take refuge in him.

Nahum 1:7 csb

In order for God to protect us, we must run to him. He is good, and he promises to offer us safety in times of trouble. However, we cannot receive his help unless we run toward him. We need to actively seek his help when trouble comes our way.

God asks you to pursue him so you will remember the true source of your strength. He is the one who created you, and he is the one who sustains you. Run to him and let him be your refuge and strength.

God, you are the true strength in my life. In times of weakness or danger, help me run to you.

Rest

It is useless for you to work so hard
from early morning until late at night,
anxiously working for food to eat;
for God gives rest to his loved ones.

Psalm 127:2 NLT

Failure to rest is usually the result of failure to trust God. There are many valid things we could do with our time, and danger comes when we forget that rest is one of them. We were created to rest, and there is no shame in taking a break from our work.

No amount of work will ever supply the deep rest that God offers. He created you with limits, and you honor him when you don't constantly push past them. He promises to give you rest when you lean on him.

Lord, I know I need rest. Give me the courage to make time for rest even when I think I'm too busy.

If you are surrendered to God, he will keep you safe.

Finished Work

I am sure of this, that he who began a good work in you will bring it to completion at the day of Jesus Christ.

PHILIPPIANS 1:6 ESV

Sometimes we want instant gratification. We want to see immediate rewards for our hard work. In our age of convenience and technology, everything is available at the click of a button. When this becomes the norm, we can project this mentality onto every aspect of our lives.

Your relationship with God and your growth as a person are not linear. You won't always be able to track your progress in a concise way, but God promises to finish the work he began in your life.

God, help me to be patient with the process and know that you're transforming me to be more like Jesus.

Nothing at All

Who can separate us from the love of Christ? Can affliction or distress or persecution or famine or nakedness or danger or sword?

Romans 8:35 CSB

It's difficult to comprehend the steadiness of Christ's covenant love. We are so prone to fickle-minded behavior that it's hard to understand something that never changes. Christ's love is the same all the time, and nothing or no one can take it away from us.

Christ's love for you has nothing to do with your behavior or circumstances. It doesn't even depend on whether or not you believe in it. Lean on the promise of Christ's love and you will remain surefooted upon a foundation that cannot be moved.

God, give me fresh understanding of your covenant love. Help me lean on your faithfulness more than my own abilities.

Working in You

God is working in you, giving you the desire and the power to do what pleases him.

PHILIPPIANS 2:13 ESV

God does not give us a list of demands and leave us to sort it out. He uses his power to help us. He equips us to live the right way, and he faithfully walks beside us. He transforms our hearts, and he gives us what we need.

God will not ask you to do anything that he hasn't already equipped you for. He joyfully gives you everything you need to please him and honor his name. Draw close to him and be strengthened by his promise to work in you and through you.

Lord, help me realize that you are the source of the daily strength I need to live for you.

Identity

You are no longer a slave but a son, and if a son, then God has made you an heir.

GALATIANS 4:7 CSB

Trusting in Christ's work on the cross changes our identity. Believing in him takes us from slaves to sons. We don't follow him around out of obligation but instead walk side by side with him as he calls us his own.

You are a son of God. That title cannot be taken away from you, and you cannot do anything to earn it. Your sonship doesn't come from anything you've done; it comes from your Father. He declares that you are his, and he sets you free from the bondage of slavery.

Thank you, God, for calling me son and smiling on me.

The more time you spend in God's presence, the more you will understand his will.

Promised Presence

"My presence will go with you, and I will give you rest." And he said to him, "If your presence will not go with me, do not bring us up from here."

Exodus 33:14-15 ESV

God promises his presence to his people. Scripture is filled with situations where God's followers face varying difficult situations, but one thing never changes. He is with them through every high and low.

Life will not always go the way you want. You will experience triumphs and disappointments. You will face suffering and inexpressible joy. While you can't change or control every detail of your life, you can depend on God's steadiness. He promises to be with you in every season.

God, thank you for the promise of your presence.

Perfect Protection

Even when I go through the darkest valley,
I fear no danger, for you are with me;
your rod and your staff—they comfort me.

Psalm 23:4 CSB

Sometimes we focus too much on the gentle and comforting image of God, forgetting that one of the primary jobs of a shepherd is to be a defender. God is our capable and committed defender. He protects every sheep within his flock.

Your heavenly Father has every intention of protecting you, and that fact should bring you deep peace. Instead of allowing fear to stir up shame, see it as an opportunity to glorify the Lord. Look to him with confidence.

God, thank you for protecting me. I can take great comfort in knowing you are with me, and you are powerful.

Peace and Strength

The Lord gives his people strength.
The Lord blesses them with peace.

Psalm 29:11 NLT

Strength and peace are often thought of as coming from within. While it's true that we experience those things internally, the source of them is both external and eternal. God gives us strength, and he blesses us with peace.

When you go through challenging times, you might be tempted to muster up the strength to carry on. You might try to manufacture your own peace or look for your own reasons to be happy. Don't forget that those things come from God, and he has an endless supply.

God, you are the source of all I need, and I am grateful.

Experience

Taste and see that the Lord is good.
How happy is the person who takes refuge in him!
You who are his holy ones, fear the Lord,
for those who fear him lack nothing.

Psalm 34:8-9 CSB

Those who fear God lack nothing. What does it mean to fear God? It means recognizing who he is and who we are in relation to him. It means acknowledging his glory and humbly receiving his mercy. It means trusting his authority and abiding in his love.

Happiness and contentment come from fearing God. As you seek him, you will find that he is the source of everything you need. Devote yourself to the pursuit of him and your soul will be satisfied.

God, I want to experience more of you. In you there is no fear and no shortage. You are good.

God has an endless well of resources that bring life, vitality, and security.

Infinitely More

All glory to God, who is able, through his mighty power at work within us, to accomplish infinitely more than we might ask or think.

EPHESIANS 3:20 NLT

Like a father building an incredible treehouse for his child or a husband unveiling a dream vacation to his wife, God takes joy in doing things for us that exceed our expectations. He wants us to look at him in wonder and realize that he is so much more impressive than we give him credit for.

God is infinitely better than you can understand. His power, goodness, and love surpass anything you can imagine. Put your faith in him and he will exceed your expectations.

God, help me to remember that you are at work in my life to create something better than I could ever create on my own.

Give Him Control

"I am the vine; you are the branches. The one who remains in me and I in him produces much fruit, because you can do nothing without me."

John 15:5 CSB

God promises that we will produce fruit if we remain in him. We cannot drum up our own success, and we cannot orchestrate the details of our lives. God alone can direct us according to his goodness and sovereignty.

Loosen your grip and give up the control you've stubbornly held on to. Lean on the Lord and let him worry about your productivity and success. Put him first and you will naturally produce the fruit you long for.

God, thank you for being my source of strength. Help me turn to you in every situation.

The Lord's Prayer

"Give us this day our daily bread, and forgive us our debts, as we also have forgiven our debtors. And lead us not into temptation, but deliver us from evil."

MATTHEW 6:11-13 ESV

God offers us freedom from temptation. We are not trapped by sin, and failure is not inevitable. Just because we come up against something powerful doesn't mean that God's strength within us isn't more powerful.

You have what it takes to stand strong in the face of temptation. As a child of God, you are fully equipped to make choices that honor him. He strengthens you when you are weak, and he gives you what you need to persevere.

God, you are good! Thank you for inviting me to come before you and pray with confidence.

Wisdom

With God are wisdom and might;
he has counsel and understanding.
Job 12:13 ESV

God has the counsel we need. He alone is the perfect judge, and he alone understands the nuances of every situation we face.

Decision making becomes an act of worship when you rely on God to lead the way. Including him in the details of your days, no matter how mundane or monumental, shows that you depend on him. Your willingness to surrender to his ways shows that you believe his promise to sustain you.

God, thank you for your guidance and wisdom. Help me to make decisions that honor you.

Your position in God's family is secure.

Loving Discipline

"The Lord disciplines those he loves, and he punishes each one he accepts as his child."

HEBREWS 12:6 NLT

God disciplines his children out of love. He offers kind correction and merciful conviction. He leads us because he knows what is best for us, and he longs for us to experience the goodness of his presence.

God's promise of discipline can be a source of reassurance for you. If you give him your life, he will help you stay on the right track. He will guide you, correct you, and teach you. He will help you grow because he loves you and knows what's best for you.

Father, I am thankful for your discipline. Thank you for helping me make corrections when I've wandered down the wrong path.

Confidence

This is the confidence that we have toward him, that if we ask anything according to his will he hears us.

1 JOHN 5:14 ESV

Men are expected to be confident, but what does that confidence look like? Fake it until we make it? Speak louder than the other guy? Quiet confidence comes from knowing who we are and trusting God as our Father. It comes from understanding God's will and aligning our lives with his purposes.

When you pray confidently, you enter the throne room of heaven. Bring your requests before the God of the universe, knowing that he hears you. The more time you spend in his presence and reading his Word, the more you will understand his will.

God, help me to pray bold prayers filled with faith. Thank you for your promise that if I pray, you will listen.

Future

Beloved, we are God's children now, and what we will be has not yet appeared; but we know that when he appears we shall be like him, because we shall see him as he is.

1 John 3:2 ESV

When Jesus ascended to heaven, he promised he would come back. He promised to return and make all things right. He will bring God's kingdom fully to earth, and we will see him face to face. He will rule and reign, and we will be fully transformed into his likeness.

Knowing that Jesus is coming back can help you persevere through life's trials. There is no pain that will last forever, and there is no suffering that can take that hope away from you. Perfection is coming because Jesus will faithfully keep his promise.

Lord Jesus, help me cling to your promise of restoration when I am overwhelmed.

Speaking Life

"Don't be afraid," he said, "for you are very precious to God. Peace! Be encouraged! Be strong!" As he spoke these words to me, I suddenly felt stronger and said to him, "Please speak to me, my lord, for you have strengthened me."

DANIEL 10:19 NLT

God's words bring life. When we actively search for what he is speaking to us, we will find a vitality we might otherwise miss.

Lift your eyes to the Lord and remember that he is on your side. He is with you at all times, and he has what you need. He calls you to be unafraid because he is the one who fights your battles. He calls you to be strong and generously offers you his strength.

God, thank you for speaking life into me. Your words have the power to heal, direct, and strengthen.

You can be as close to God as you want to be.

Transparency

If we confess our sins, he is faithful and just to forgive us our sins and to cleanse us from all unrighteousness.

1 John 1:9 ESV

God promises us forgiveness when we admit our wrongdoing. He doesn't ask us to fix everything, clean up our mess, or even change our behavior. The first thing he asks us to do is have enough humility to acknowledge we are wrong.

When you confess your sins, God forgives. He cleanses you and strengthens you to go on. He gives you wisdom to navigate whatever situation you are in, and he helps you heal whatever is wounded. It all begins with confession.

Lord Jesus, teach me humility and help me lean on your mercy. Give me the courage to confess my sins.

Endless Supply

He who did not spare his own Son but gave him up for us all, how will he not also with him graciously give us all things?

Romans 8:32 esv

Discouragement, loneliness, and despair can find their way into our lives. The one thing we can be assured of in those seasons is that God is continuously faithful to his people. He did not hesitate in giving his own Son to die on our behalf.

God has an endless well of resources that bring life, vitality, and security. When the world strips you of hope and security, he is the balm that brings restoration to the soul.

Lord Jesus, forgive me when I doubt the sufficiency of your love. Teach me to trust that you always hold me in your hand.

Always at Work

The LORD opened the eyes of the young man, and he saw. And behold, the mountain was full of horses and chariots of fire all around Elisha.

2 KINGS 6:17 NKJV

Sight and vision are not the same. Just because we can see with our physical eyes doesn't mean that we have the spiritual vision to understand how God is moving. He operates in ways that we don't always notice. He is always moving on behalf of his people even if we don't see it.

Ask God to show you how he is moving in your life. Physical circumstances might not always meet your expectations, but everything looks different from God's vantage point. He is always at work, and he won't stop intervening on your behalf.

God, give me your vision to see things your way. Encourage me when my circumstances feel challenging.

Deliverance

I sought the Lord, and he answered me
and delivered me from all my fears.
Psalm 34:4 ESV

God delivers his people. He helps those in need and pursues those who are lost. He offers his strong arms to the weak, and he is compassionate toward the broken. He notices the oppressed and lifts up those who are overlooked. He is a place of refuge and a strong tower for everyone who calls on his name.

Seek the Lord and he will answer you. Look to him and he will strengthen you. He does not want you to be afraid, ashamed, embarrassed, or defeated. He longs to care for you, and he promises to respond when you call out to him.

Father God, may I be known as a man who seeks you. I need you and your deliverance today.

God sees you, and he knows what you need.

Know God

"Truly, truly, I say to you, the Son can do nothing of his own accord, but only what he sees the Father doing. For whatever the Father does, that the Son does likewise."

John 5:19 ESV

God is not a mystery that we cannot solve. He is not hiding from us or withholding himself. He has given us a perfect picture of who he is. If we want to know God, we simply need to look at Jesus. Jesus is a perfect reflection of the Father.

You can know and understand God through Jesus. Learn about his life and become familiar with his character. Study his ways and pay attention to the things he said. His behavior tells you everything you need to know about God.

Lord Jesus, thank you for showing me the Father. Thank you for making a way for me to be with him.

Recreated

You are no longer strangers and aliens, but you are fellow citizens with the saints and members of the household of God, built on the foundation of the apostles and prophets, Christ Jesus himself being the cornerstone.

EPHESIANS 2:19-20 ESV

In Christ, everything has changed. We were once strangers to the things of God, but now we have been grafted into his kingdom. We are members of his family because we have been adopted through the blood of Jesus.

Your position in God's family is secure. You are no longer a stranger to him. You are an heir, and your place at his table is promised. You don't have to wonder where you belong, and you don't have to navigate life alone. As a follower of Jesus, you stand securely on a foundation that cannot be shaken.

Father, thank you that I am an insider in your family.

Righteousness of Christ

God made him who had no sin to be sin for us, so that in him we might become the righteousness of God.

2 Corinthians 5:21 NIV

Righteousness is being in right standing before the Lord. The great unifying problem of humanity is that no one is righteous. No one can compare to God's perfection. No one can claim to be blameless.

Your lack of righteousness is certain, but Jesus is your Redeemer! He offers you his righteousness. His death and resurrection made a way for you to be blameless before God. Jesus didn't sin, and he advocates for you even though you have sinned. Your righteousness is promised through Christ.

God, thank you for making me blameless through Christ's sacrifice.

Overcomers

Little children, you are from God and have overcome them, for he who is in you is greater than he who is in the world.

1 John 4:4 ESV

Overcoming is natural in the life of the believer. We overcome when we don't give up on our faith, refuse to live in fear, and continue to obey. We overcome when we remember that Jesus in us is greater than any force in the world. Victory is certain when we remain in Christ.

God within you is greater than any problem you might face. He is capable of handling any situation, and he is stronger than any of your enemies. You can take each step with confidence because you know that God is on your side.

Lord Jesus, thank you for making me an overcomer. You are greater than anything I am facing.

God has given you the gift of belonging.

Anxiety Steals

Do not be anxious about anything, but in everything by prayer and supplication with thanksgiving let your request be made known to God.

PHILIPPIANS 4:6 ESV

The world is full of anxiety. There is suffering, disappointment, and conflict everywhere we turn. He is aware of every trial and frustration we face. He is not surprised by the state of the world, and he has given us everything we need to walk with peace and contentment.

Your heart can be light even when your burdens are heavy. God himself promises to help you. Offer him your trials and thank him for his blessings. Put your life in his hands and trust that he knows what to do.

Lord Jesus, forgive me for not trusting you. Fill me with hope and help me lean on your strength.

Wisdom from Above

If any of you lacks wisdom, he should ask God—
who gives to all generously and ungrudgingly—
and it will be given to him.

James 1:5 CSB

Life is full of uncertainty. We don't know what tomorrow will look like, and we don't know if our plans will work out the way we imagine. We don't know what trials we'll face, and we don't know what gifts we'll be blessed with. In the midst of all the unknown, there are certain things we can always count on. Wisdom is one of them.

If you ask God for wisdom, he will give it to you. He promises to do it, and you can count on his Word. He does not withhold wisdom from those who ask for it.

Father, thank you for the promise of wisdom.

Finding Hope Again

Those who sow with tears will reap with songs of joy.
Those who go out weeping, carrying seed to sow,
will return with songs of joy, carrying sheaves with them.

PSALM 126:5-6 NIV

God takes his time to accomplish his work. He doesn't promise us a timeline that matches our expectations, but he does promise us particular outcomes. If we tearfully call upon him, he will give us joy. He responds to us as we devote our lives to him.

If you are used to carrying burdens alone, it might feel foreign to surrender to God. Offer him your most desperate prayers, and he will meet you.

God, fill me with patience as I wait for you. I trust you with the timeline of my life.

Living by Faith

Without faith it is impossible to please him, for whoever would draw near to God must believe that he exists and that he rewards those who seek him.

HEBREWS 11:6 ESV

Faith pleases God. Your simple and consistent belief in him gives him joy. He is proud of you when you acknowledge him and try to honor him. You can't follow his ways without the foundation of unshakable belief.

Your belief in God's existence matters, but you must also believe in his character. He rewards you for seeking him. If you are confident in his promises, he will be pleased by your faith.

God, thank you for the goodness of your character. Help me trust you more.

If you walk in God's ways, he will light your path.

Promised Provision

Know that the Lord, he is God!
It is he who made us, and we are his;
we are his people, and the sheep of his pasture.

Psalm 100:3 ESV

God is our shepherd, and we can trust him to take care of us. A shepherd knows what his sheep need, he defends them, and he guides them. He gives them a home, and he sustains them.

You can put your confidence in the promise of God's provision. He sees you, and he knows what you need. He is aware of how hard you work, and he knows the burdens you carry. He longs to give you peace in his presence.

God, thank you for leading me and providing for me. I trust you with the details of my life.

Wandering Soul

All of us, like sheep, have strayed away. We have left God's paths to follow our own. Yet the LORD laid on him the sins of us all.

ISAIAH 53:6 NLT

For the most part, we are all aware of our flaws. We know that we are lacking, and we feel our failures to our core. We struggle to live how we want, and we battle against our flesh. It's realistic to be acutely aware of our sin, but we must also be acutely aware of our salvation.

God has laid your sins upon Jesus. He has guided you back to his heart, and he has made you clean. He has rescued you from your own failures, and he has called you his own. No matter how many times you wander from his path, you can find your way back to through Christ.

Jesus, thank you for bearing my sins. Draw me back to you whenever I begin to wander away.

Always Working

We know that God causes everything to work together for the good of those who love God and are called according to his purpose for them.

Romans 8:28 NLT

Scripture offers us hope in the midst of negative circumstances. As Christians, we believe that God is moving in ways that we can't see and might not understand. He is capable of taking difficult situations and using them for his glory.

God is working even when your health is poor, your job is in jeopardy, and your relationships are a struggle. He is working all the time, and you can depend on his ability to be faithful.

God, help me trust you even when things are difficult. You are always in control.

Belonging

Even before he made the world, God loved us and chose us in Christ to be holy and without fault in his eyes. God decided in advance to adopt us into his own family by bringing us to himself through Jesus Christ. This is what he wanted to do, and it gave him great pleasure.

EPHESIANS 1:4-5 NLT

God is pleased to bring us into his family. He doesn't rescue us out of obligation, and he doesn't begrudgingly redeem us. He gathers us in because he wants to.

God has given you the gift of belonging. You are part of his family. You are his son, and he is delighted to be near you. He wants to be close to you. Even when you feel out of place or alone in this world, you can find value and belonging in his presence.

God, thank you for the gift of belonging. Thank you for the promise of acceptance through Jesus.

The true measure of your strength is found in God.

Power of Speech

The tongue can bring death or life;
those who love to talk will reap the consequences.

PROVERBS 18:21 NLT

We often underestimate the power of our words, and we forget that they can have a lasting impact. When we pay attention to what we say, we can heal the hurting, restore the weary, and create community.

A loose lip can lead to division and destruction. Those who love to talk will experience the consequences of their carelessness. Speak words of love and life instead.

God, help me be quick to listen and slow to speak. Help me use my words wisely to affirm and build others up.

Constant Companion

When you believed in Christ, he identified you as his own by giving you the Holy Spirit, whom he promised long ago. The Spirit is God's guarantee that he will give us the inheritance he promised and that he has purchased us to be his own people.

EPHESIANS 1:13-14 NLT

We have all been promised the gift of the Holy Spirit. God knew that we would need help navigating the difficulties of life, and he ensured that we would not get lost along the way. He gave us a helper, advocate, comforter, and friend.

There might be times in life when you feel lost, but you have the Spirit to help you. His job is to transform, equip, and encourage you. He reminds you of the truth, and he gives you wisdom when you need it. He is a constant companion.

God, awaken my soul and help me follow the Spirit's leading.

Fearless

There is no fear in love, but perfect love casts out fear. For fear has to do with punishment, and whoever fears has not been perfected in love.

1 John 4:18 ESV

God's love makes us fearless. We are fearless as we face death, and we are fearless as we face life. We are empowered to face anything that comes our way because God is our strength.

If you feel enslaved to a particular fear, let the love of God empower you. Whether you're afraid of something physical or a certain set of circumstances, God wants to strengthen you and encourage you. He will faithfully stay by your side despite your fears.

Father, thank you for your love. Remind me who I am. Help me stand strong in the face of fear.

Mighty to Save

Be strong in the Lord and in the strength of his might. Put on the whole armor of God, that you may be able to stand against the schemes of the devil.

EPHESIANS 6:10-11 ESV

At some point, we discover that life is more like a battleground than a playground. We encounter tests and tough times and may even feel like we're under attack. Paul reminds us to call upon God for strength even when our circumstances are desolate.

God does not leave you defenseless in the battles you face. He gives you armor, and he equips you with weapons of truth, righteousness, peace, faith, and salvation. Call upon the Lord in your time of trouble, for he is mighty to save.

Lord, you are stronger than all of my enemies. I trust you to save me.

God offers you the abundant life your soul longs for.

Soul Satisfaction

The Lord is my shepherd;
I have all that I need.
Psalm 23:1 NLT

We see billboards along the highway, advertisements in the paper, and banners on our screens all tempting us to buy something new. The world has a way of convincing us that something is missing. We become trapped in an endless cycle of fulfilling our desires and moving on to the next thing.

True fulfillment cannot come from what you have. Soul-level satisfaction comes from God alone. If you are searching for your own version of happiness, you will never find it. Instead, look toward the Good Shepherd and remember that you have everything you need.

God, simplify my desires. Thank you for your gracious and generous provision.

Guidance

Your word is a lamp to my feet
and a light to my path.
Psalm 119:105 ESV

Most of us like to have control. We want to know where we are going and how we will get there. We want God to reveal a clear path, and we want to know which obstacles we'll face along the way. The reality is that we are never in control. God alone sees the trajectory of our days, and we must choose to trust him.

God has given you his Word to illuminate your steps. He promises that if you walk in his ways, he will light your path. He will faithfully show you each step you need to take.

God, as you light the next steps of my journey, give me the courage to walk in your ways.

Masterpiece

We are God's masterpiece. He has created us anew in Christ Jesus, so we can do the good things he planned for us long ago.

Ephesians 2:10 NLT

Our lives are not made up of random events pieced together. We were created with intention and purpose by the hands of God. Our very existence speaks to the intricate creativity that God possesses. He alone can create life, and he alone sustains it.

You are God's masterpiece. He formed you in your mother's womb, and he gave you life again when you chose to follow him. You have a purpose, and your days matter. God has prepared good works for you, and he has equipped you to accomplish them.

God, open my eyes to see what makes me unique. Help me discover my role in your kingdom.

Slow to Anger

He is so rich in kindness and grace that he purchased our freedom with the blood of his Son and forgave our sins.

EPHESIANS 1:7 NLT

It's typical to imagine God as mighty, powerful, and motivated by justice. We don't have much difficulty imagining him on a glorious throne, ruling and reigning. It's important that we recognize that he is equally kind and gracious. He is strong and wise, but he is also gentle, attentive, and tender.

God promises to be kind to you. He longs to empower you with his grace. He is patient, slow to anger, and compassionate. Run to him whenever you need him and expect him to be kind.

God, help me tap into your great big heart and abundant resources. You are the source of everything I need.

God offers the gift of eternal salvation to all who call on his name.

Pilgrimage

Blessed are those whose strength is in you,
whose hearts are set on pilgrimage.
PSALM 84:5 NIV

Our lives are consumed by whatever we think is most important. The way we spend our time, energy, and money shows us the desires of our hearts. Blessing comes from seeking the Lord above all else.

Set your heart on a pilgrimage toward Jesus and pursue something that is bigger than yourself. God promises that blessing will be yours when you devote your life to his promises and purposes.

Father, I don't want to settle for lesser things or smaller goals. I want your plans to be my plans.

Prevailing Purpose

You can make many plans,
but the LORD*'s purpose will prevail.*
PROVERBS 19:21 NLT

Planning helps us prepare for the unknown. It provides a sense of stability as we journey through life, but sometimes we need to let go of our plans. It's more important that we hold our expectations loosely and put our trust in the Lord.

There is no question as to whether or not God will accomplish his purposes. It's set in stone. He will be victorious in the end. Don't bet on your own flawed perspective when you can plant your feet firmly in God's immovable will.

God, I open my hands and heart to joyfully receive the purpose you have for me.

Rise Again

Do not gloat over me, my enemies!
For though I fall, I will rise again.
Though I sit in darkness, the LORD will be my light.

MICAH 7:8 NLT

Our strength is not measured by how many times we fail. It is not calculated by the number of mistakes we make or the amount of losses we accumulate. The true measure of our strength is found in the Lord. When we put our hope in him, there is no limit to the amount of times we can rise again.

You can fail with confidence when the Lord is the source of your strength. You can sit in the darkness, knowing that the light of the Lord shines brightest in dark times. He promises to lift you up no matter how many times you fall.

God, be my strength and my light. Help me to keep my eyes on you no matter what is happening around me.

Embracing Abundance

"A thief comes only to steal and kill and destroy. I have come so that they may have life and have it in abundance."

JOHN 10:10 CSB

There are seasons when we struggle just to get by. There are also seasons when we are lulled into complacency by the mundane details of life. Something deep within us knows that we were created for more.

You are most at home in the presence of the Lord. He offers you abundant life that cannot come from anything else. There isn't a goal you can reach or a glimmer of happiness you can chase that compares to the joy found in him.

God, give me a heart that desires the abundant life you offer.

Jesus came to bring you life.

58

No Longer Anxious

"I tell you, do not be anxious about your life, what you will eat or what you will drink, nor about your body, what you will put on."

MATTHEW 6:25 ESV

Life is filled with reasons to cling to anxiety. We find things to worry about and often perceive little things as big problems. If we take the time to understand the real issue and whose hand we hold as we journey, we will experience peace that settles our souls.

Jesus offers you peace when you cannot find it anywhere else. He will faithfully take care of you for all your days. He has not overlooked you, and he will not abandon you. He knows exactly what you need down to the tiniest detail, and it is his great joy to provide for you.

God, may your provision bring me peace and your faithfulness calm my fears.

Like a Child

"Truly I tell you, anyone who will not receive the kingdom of God like a little child will never enter it."

MARK 10:15 NIV

We see God when we become like little children. We are promised to understand heavenly things when we embrace the simplicity and innocence of our faith. Children are dependent on their father and believe what he says.

If you want to embrace child-like faith, you'll need to lay down your pride. Adamantly refuse to cultivate a faith that depends on your own wisdom, strength, or fortitude. God's ways are higher than yours. Receive his kingdom like a child, and you will enter it.

God, help me become like a child so I can receive the kingdom with awe and wonder.

Trust in the Lord

Trust in the LORD with all your heart,
and do not lean on your own understanding.
In all your ways acknowledge him,
and he will make straight your paths.

PROVERBS 3:5-6 ESV

We experience life differently when we trust God with half a heart or lean on our own understanding. The biggest difference is our level of anxiety. When we get swept up in the conflict and confusion of the day, our paths get crisscrossed, and we lose our way.

Self-reliance is not your only option. God invites you to depend on him. He wants to make your path straight. Follow him and trust in his ways. Give him your anxiety, and he will keep your steps steady.

Lord, thank you for the opportunity to depend on you. Help me trust you even when I don't understand.

More than Mundane

"Everyone who drinks of this water will be thirsty again, but whoever drinks of the water that I will give him will never be thirsty again. The water that I will give him will become in him a spring of water welling up to eternal life."

JOHN 4:13-14 ESV

Our daily routines can condition us into comfortable living. We settle for repeated rhythms and expect our lives to change. Day after day, month after month, year after year, we find life in the things that satisfy only our immediate needs and desires. Our hearts long for so much more, but we settle for so much less.

Christ offers you the abundant life your soul longs for. Let Jesus disrupt your daily patterns of living, and your eyes will be opened to the goodness of following him.

God, thank you for the abundant goodness and eternal treasures you offer me.

God is on your side.

Glorious Riches

This same God who takes care of me will supply all your needs from his glorious riches, which have been given to us in Christ Jesus.

Philippians 4:19 NLT

Each of us can make a lengthy list of the things we think we need. We all have different standards and preferences when it comes to comfort and convenience.

God promises to meet your needs. He promised to supply your needs from his glorious riches. This doesn't mean that he will grant your every wish or make your life seamless. It does mean that if you rely on him, he will provide for you. It is his joy to take care of you because you are his beloved son.

God, may I be a man who seeks you first. I trust in your faithfulness, and I believe you won't let me down.

When Striving Ceases

"Stop fighting, and know that I am God, exalted among the nations, exalted on the earth."

Psalm 46:10 CSB

Godly men are held to a high standard. Work harder, lead better, love sacrificially, and be stronger. The pressure lies on our shoulders. If we attempt to do all those things on our own, we will surely fall. We must give up our striving, and rest in the presence of our Maker.

When strivings cease, God's power is evident. When you are weak, he is strong. Take a step back from your immediate struggles and stand in awe of the one who holds it all together.

God, may your name be exalted in my life. May your purposes outshine my own.

Aligned Desires

Take delight in the LORD,
and he will give you your heart's desires.
Commit everything you do to the LORD.
Trust him, and he will help you.

PSALM 37:4-5 NLT

Something unique happens when we delight in God. As we look to him, he starts to plant new desires within us. He gives us a hunger for more of his presence and character. If we delight in God, he will start to shape our desires to be in alignment with his.

Time spent with God will strengthen your commitment to him. True commitment to him will bring about wisdom, grace, and perspective for whatever comes your way.

God, I commit myself and my desires to you. Help me to align myself with your will.

Promised Ending

After this I saw a vast crowd, too great to count, from every nation and tribe and people and language, standing in front of the throne and before the Lamb.

Revelation 7:9 NIV

When John got a glimpse of heaven, he saw people from all continents, people groups, and economic backgrounds worshiping Jesus. God offers the gift of eternal salvation to all who call upon his name. He does not discriminate, and he is not biased.

No one who seeks Jesus while living will be overlooked in eternity. His kingdom will be filled to the brim with multitudes of people. If you give him your life now, you will be among the masses on that glorious day.

God, thank you for the beautiful ending to your story. Thank you for the victory I have in you.

God is not surprised by your circumstances, and he will not leave your side.

Highest Priority

"I give you a new command: Love one another. Just as I have loved you, you are also to love one another. By this everyone will know that you are my disciples, if you love one another."

John 13:34-35 CSB

Loving others is meant to be our highest priority. It is how the world will recognize that we are followers of Jesus. Our rules, traditions, and laws don't matter nearly as much as our ability to lay our lives down for the people around us. People see Jesus when we choose to be kind, thoughtful, and servant-hearted.

Loving the people around you is rarely convenient, easy, or simple, but it is worth it. Love others and they will see Jesus.

Heavenly Father, fill my heart and soul with your love so I can love others more generously.

He Sees You

The Lord your God is with you,
the Mighty Warrior who saves.
He will take great delight in you;
in his love he will no longer rebuke you,
but will rejoice over you with singing.

Zephaniah 3:17 niv

God is not far away. He isn't disinterested, and he doesn't ignore our plights. He is so happy that we are his children. We delight him, and he is eager to walk with us through our days. He cares about the details of our lives, and he notices us when we are troubled.

God sees you. You are not overlooked or ignored. You might go through seasons where you feel as though you are fighting alone, but he is with you every step of the way.

God, thank you for the nearness of your presence. Help me lean on your faithfulness when trials come my way.

What Really Matters

"Store your treasures in heaven, where moths and rust cannot destroy, and thieves do not break in and steal. Wherever your treasure is, there the desires of your heart will also be."

MATTHEW 6:20-21 NLT

It's so easy to fall into the trap of wanting things. Our culture is fueled by persuasive marketing, and we are constantly being told that we don't have enough. If we aren't careful, we begin to believe that the remedy for our discontent is just one purchase away.

Take time to think about how you view money and possessions. What does your lifestyle say about who you are and where your allegiance lies? Give your time, energy, and resources to the things that really matter, and you won't be disappointed.

God, protect me from the love of money. Help me to put my trust in you even more today.

True Rest

"Take my yoke upon you and learn from me, because I am lowly and humble in heart, and you will find rest for your souls."

MATTHEW 11:29 CSB

Life alone is exhausting, but Jesus offers us another way. When we are yoked with him, he carries our burdens. He longs to take each step alongside us, lifting the loads we cannot bear.

Yoke yourself to Jesus, and you will not be alone. Walk beside him, shoulder to shoulder, and remember that his strength is sufficient for you. Your circumstances might still be difficult, but your ability to navigate them is shifted by the faithfulness of Jesus.

God, teach me to walk in your ways. May I experience rest as you draw me into your presence.

You have everything you need to live a godly life.

At Your Worst

God shows his love for us in that while we were still sinners, Christ died for us.

Romans 5:8 esv

We are undeserving of Christ's humble sacrifice. Not one of us have lived a life that is good enough for God's standard of perfection. We all fall short. The beauty of Jesus' love is that he offers it despite our weaknesses.

Entitlement is dangerous. No matter how many rules you've followed or how many successes you've had, you are not perfect. Humbly acknowledge your downfalls and stand in awe of Christ's sacrifice. He saw you at your worst, and he offered you mercy.

Lord Jesus, forgive me for being prideful. Help me embrace a life of humility and sacrifice.

Well Connected

In Christ we can come before God with freedom and without fear. We can do this through faith in Christ.

EPHESIANS 3:12 NCV

We all want to be that guy who has the connection to courtside seats at the big game, or the one who has the ear of the boss at work. The connections we make often come with benefits. How quickly we forget that we have direct access to God.

You have freedom to be with God because of what Jesus did on the cross. You have a guaranteed audience with him because of Christ's sacrifice. Through Jesus you have the most powerful connection you'll ever need.

God, thank you that I don't need an appointment or even a reason to come to you. Thank you for listening to me.

In Control

"Seek first his kingdom and his righteousness, and all these things will be given to you as well."

MATTHEW 6:33 NIV

We are wired to provide for the people we love. We want to take care of others, and we want to be strong enough to meet their needs. We worry about being enough and doing enough. It's so important to remember that we are not the end of the line.

Provision might come through us, but God is the one who orchestrates it. He is in control. He deserves honor and praise for every good thing that happens in your life. He ultimately sustains you and gives you what we need. Seek him first, and he will make sure that you are taken care of.

God, thank you for my daily bread. Help me to trust that you will provide for me.

No Shame

There is now no condemnation for those who are in Christ Jesus, because through Christ Jesus the law of the Spirit who gives life has set you free from the law of sin and death.

ROMANS 8:1-2 NIV

We all make mistakes. Something beautiful about the Christian life is that we are no longer defined by our failures. Our worth and identity come from Jesus, and we are encouraged to put more confidence in his ability than our own.

The way you respond to failure is so much more important than the mistakes you make. Admit your wrongdoing with humility and call upon the Lord for mercy. Ask him for forgiveness. He promises to give you mercy and grace when you need it most.

God, grant me grace for every situation I encounter today. When I fail, lift my eyes to look at you.

God offers you his ear,
and his perspective
is flawless.

Seen and Healed

"It is not the healthy who need a doctor, but the sick. I have not come to call the righteous, but sinners."

Mark 2:17 NIV

Can you imagine a hospital filled with people who don't need a doctor? Obvious ailments need obvious solutions. This is why Jesus used this example with his disciples. He wants us to see our desperate need and recognize that he provides the cure.

We are all in the same boat; we fall short of God's glory and are lost in our weakness and sin. But God has promised to heal us. He is our great physician, and he generously mends all who come to him with their brokenness.

Father, I confess my need for you again today. I trust you to heal what is broken in my life.

Called and Equipped

Loving God means keeping his commandments, and his commandments are not burdensome.

1 John 5:3 NLT

God doesn't ask his people to be overwhelmed, stressed out, and weary. He doesn't ask us to trudge through life or grit our teeth through the trials. He asks us to follow his commandments, but he reassures us that it's not meant to be burdensome. He teaches us how to live, and he gives us everything we need to do it.

Jesus came to bring you life. He came so you would know freedom, love, and the abundance of his goodness. He longs to lighten your heart and give you rest.

God, forgive me for the times that I've insisted on carrying my own burdens. Thank you for the rest you offer.

On Your Side

"The LORD is on my side; I will not fear.
What can man do to me?"
PSALM 118:6 ESV

Fear can be packaged in many ways. Sometimes it might look like anxiety over sickness or financial instability. Sometimes it might come from past experiences. Sometimes our fears are irrational and even fabricated. Despite the varying ways fear can show up, we have a consistent antidote; God is on our side.

When everything feels messy, circumstances don't fit your expectations, and the world is filled with chaos and turmoil, God is on your side. He is faithful and strong through every season and every trial.

God, help me to recognize that fear cannot be sustained in the blinding light of your presence.

Poor in Spirit

"Blessed are the poor in spirit,
for theirs is the kingdom of heaven."
MATTHEW 5:3 NIV

Being poor in spirit has nothing to do with financial security or physical circumstances. We are poor in spirit when we acknowledge our desperate need for salvation, when we are acutely aware of our depravity, and when we know that we cannot rely on our own skills, talents, or possessions to save us.

The beauty of this promise is that you will experience great blessing when you recognize how much you lack. True happiness doesn't come from a multitude of things, but from seeing your desperate need for God. Call out to him from a place of weakness, and he will lift you up.

God, remind me of my need for you and keep me from letting pride slip into my heart.

You have been made complete.

Persistent Prayer

"Keep on asking, and you will receive what you ask for. Keep on seeking, and you will find. Keep on knocking, and the door will be opened to you. For everyone who asks, receives. Everyone who seeks, finds. And to everyone who knocks, the door will be opened."

MATTHEW 7:7-8 NLT

In the kingdom of God, persistence equals success. We are promised that we will find God whenever we look for him. There is great joy in fortitude and perseverance.

God answers prayers. He doesn't always answer how you expect, but he does answer. He promises you his presence, and he always keeps his word. Your persistence displays your faith, and it is pleasing to the Lord.

God, give me confidence to approach you with boldness and perseverance when I want to give up.

How to Be Great

"It should not be that way among you. Whoever wants to become great among you must serve the rest of you like a servant."

MATTHEW 20:26 NCV

We all desire power, influence, and importance to some degree. At the very least, we want to know we matter. The world tells us that we must become great in order to find that feeling. We must elevate ourselves, seek our own desires, and pursue personal happiness in order to be great.

Jesus' way of living is contrary to the world. He offers you a different path, and it leads to eternal life. His path to greatness is paved by self-sacrifice and humility.

God, help me grow as a humble servant leader. Show me opportunities to lay my life down for others and give me strength to sacrifice my own comfort for those around me.

Faithful and Good

Give thanks to the Lord, for he is good.
His faithful love endures forever.

Psalm 136:1 CSB

God is always good. Our perception of him might be skewed, but that doesn't impact the steadiness of his character. He has promised us his goodness. His faithful love does not change based on our belief or disbelief.

Get to know who God is and how he moves. As you do, you'll grow in confidence of his goodness and faithfulness. Learn the ins and outs of his character and deliberately grow in your understanding of him. Seek him diligently, and your eyes will be opened to the depths of his love for you.

God, help me to be convinced of your goodness and have confidence in your character.

Always Prepared

You should know this, Timothy, that in the last days there will be very difficult times.

2 TIMOTHY 3:1 NLT

If we pay attention to Scripture, we shouldn't be surprised by difficult times. God has been faithful to warn and prepare us. The presence of suffering does not invalidate the presence of God. In fact, suffering creates a unique opportunity to depend on his strength in an even more impactful way.

Your life will not always be easy. You will face unexpected trials and grief that threaten to drown you. Remember that God is not surprised by your circumstances, and he will not leave your side. He sees every difficulty coming, and he has faithfully prepared you in ways you might not ever understand.

Heavenly Father, give me courage to face the storms of life. I trust you.

Heart Transformation

Do not conform to the pattern of this world, but be transformed by the renewing of your mind. Then you will be able to test and approve what God's will is—his good, pleasing and perfect will.

ROMANS 12:2 NIV

Society is filled with opinions about how to live. Everyone has a different idea of what success means, and the loudest voice gets the most airtime. It's easy to be distracted by the world's ideas. As Christians, we are called to live in a different way.

Honoring God's way begins with a heart transformation. Invite the Holy Spirit to move in your life and fill your mind with the truth of the Word. This is how you will learn what God's will is. Saturate your life with biblical truth and you won't be consumed by the ways of the world.

God, help me fill my mind with truth and stand strong in the face of temptation.

Strength of Nearness

Give yourselves completely to God. Stand against the devil, and the devil will run from you. Come near to God, and God will come near to you. You sinners, clean sin out of your lives. You who are trying to follow God and the world at the same time, make your thinking pure.

JAMES 4:7-8 NCV

We are not helpless in our fight against sin and death. We must believe that God has equipped us to be victorious. If we approach our sin with a defeated attitude, we won't leave room for God to move. Instead, we must remember the promise that the devil flees when we resist.

You have everything you need to live a godly life. You can honor God and stand strong against the devil. Strength is found by drawing near to God. His nearness is your most powerful, accessible, and reliable weapon.

God, thank you for the strength I find in your presence. Thank you for your promise to draw near to me as I draw near to you.

Your devotion to Christ guarantees you a place at God's table.

Good Gifts

"You fathers—if your children ask for a fish, do you give them a snake instead? Or if they as for an egg, do you give them a scorpion? Of course not! So if you sinful people know how to give good gifts to your children, how much more will your heavenly Father give the Holy Spirit to those who ask him."

LUKE 11:11-13 NLT

There is nothing like the face of a child who receives a present. Their joy is a delight. Good fathers love to give gifts to their children. It's a father's great privilege to show his children how much he loves them.

Your Father in heaven also knows how to give good gifts. In fact, he has given you the greatest gift: the Holy Spirit. If you ask him, he will consistently guide, teach, and encourage you. He will walk with you every day of your life.

God, you know exactly what I need. Thank you for showing me what good gifts are.

Faithful Confidante

He counts the number of the stars;
He calls them all by name.
Great is our Lord, and mighty in power;
His understanding is infinite.

Psalm 147:4-5 NKJV

This verse reminds us that God's understanding is infinite. There is no situation or problem that is beyond his comprehension. He sees everything perfectly even when we are lost or confused. We can approach him with confidence, knowing that he has unlimited knowledge and wisdom.

Have you ever wished you had someone to talk to who fully understood you? God offers you his ear, and his perspective is flawless. Call upon him, and you will find a faithful confidante.

God, thank you that you are understanding. Help me to trust you with my uncertainty today.

Saved by Mercy

He saved us, not because of the righteous things we had done, but because of his mercy. He washed away our sins, giving us a new birth and new life through the Holy Spirit.

Titus 3:5 NLT

Our sins have been washed away. They don't exist anymore. We know that God forgives us, but do we understand the depths of that forgiveness? Once we confess our sins and call upon Jesus' name, we are given new life.

If you have trusted in Christ's work on the cross, you are a new creation. You have been saved by mercy, and your sins have been washed away. You no longer need to feel guilt or shame for your mistakes. They have been wiped from your history by the blood of Jesus.

Jesus, thank you for mercifully cleansing me of my sin. Thank you for the power of your blood and the confidence I have in your sacrifice.

Strong Foundation

"Everyone who hears these words of mine and puts them into practice is like a wise man who built his house on the rock. The rain came down, the streams rose, and the winds blew and beat against that house; yet it did not fall, because it had its foundation on the rock."

MATTHEW 7:24-25 NIV

The foundation of our faith is built through action. It is built by taking the words of Christ and putting them into practice. The work of obedience creates a foundation that won't be shaken in the storms of life.

God doesn't ask you to follow him because he wants to be listened to. He asks you to be obedient because he knows that it will equip you to stand strong in the battles of life.

Lord, help me to be obedient to you and build my life upon your truth.

Sovereign and Sufficient

"I am the Alpha and the Omega," says the Lord God, "the one who is, who was, and who is to come, the Almighty."

REVELATION 1:8 CSB

God has always been, and he will always be. All of time is held securely in his hands. He knows every moment of the past, and he knows exactly what the future will bring. Nothing has ever happened outside of his watchful eye, and nothing ever will.

God's sovereignty is promised. You can relax, knowing that he created and sustains the universe. He is present in every corner of creation, and he is attentive to the details of your life.

God, you hold everything in your hands. I trust you because you have proven yourself faithful and worthy.

Strength in Weakness

He said to me, "My grace is sufficient for you, for my power is made perfect in weakness." Therefore I will boast all the more gladly of my weaknesses, so that the power of Christ may rest upon me.

2 Corinthians 12:9 esv

We aren't always willing to admit our weaknesses. We don't like to confess that we get lost while driving, much less that we are struggling. We are acutely aware of the people who count on us, and defeat isn't an option.

You will lead the people in your life successfully when you are willing to surrender to the Lord. Humility and teachability matter so much more than brute strength or independence. Depend on God's ability, and you will teach others to do the same.

God, forgive me for not seeking help when I need it. Help me admit my weaknesses to you today.

Look forward with hope because God's promise of perfection will be fulfilled.

Promised Help

They who wait for the LORD
shall renew their strength;
they shall mount up with wings like eagles;
they shall run and not be weary;
they shall walk and not faint.

ISAIAH 40:31 ESV

Feeling worn out should serve as a reminder to connect with God. When we trust that God is at work and we are simply assisting him, we find a deep supply of energy to keep doing his will.

The next time you're exhausted, pause and talk to God. He may encourage you to keep going, equip you to stand strong, or remind you to rest. No matter how he responds, he promises to help you keep going in a way you might have thought impossible before.

Lord, help me run to you for help, expecting that you will sustain me.

From the Heart

"A good man brings good things out of the good stored up in his heart, and an evil man brings evil things out of the evil stored up in his heart. For the mouth speaks what the heart is full of."

Luke 6:45 NIV

If we want goodness to flow from our mouths and into the lives of those around us, we need to spend time filling our hearts with good things. We cannot consume a steady diet of darkness or compromise and expect our lives to reflect God's holiness and goodness.

You can trust God with your heart and your life. He is a worthy judge, and a kind father. If you ask him to fill your life with goodness, he will help you. He will teach you how to see from his perspective, and he will equip you to follow his ways. He will give you strength to stand against evil, and he will help you embrace what he says is good.

God, open my eyes to see things from your perspective. Help me see what is good and what is evil. May I lean on your Spirit for discernment and understanding.

Lifted Up

Humble yourselves, therefore, under the mighty hand of God, so that he may exalt you at the proper time, casting all your cares on him, because he cares about you.

1 Peter 5:6-7 csb

Embracing humility is the start of developing true character and integrity. As men, we struggle with this. We want others to think we have it all together. We want to avoid weakness because we want to be seen as trustworthy and capable. But we follow Jesus who submitted himself to death on a cross because of his humility.

Being humble leads to greater trust in God. The more you recognize your weaknesses, the more you'll see his strength. He will lift you up at the right time, and he will take care of your worries.

God, I admit that I cannot do this on my own. I need you. I am not invincible. Help me trust your ways.

Rewarded

"When you give to the needy, do not let your left hand know what your right hand is doing, so that your giving may be in secret. And your Father who sees in secret will reward you."

Matthew 6:3-4 NIV

Jesus often talked about how to handle money. Giving was always a top priority for him. Generosity is easier said than done. Sometimes in our life of surrender to the Lord, our wallet is the final thing handed over.

God asks you to be generous, and he promises to reward you. He doesn't want you to give because you're obligated to; he wants you to give because he has already given so much to you. Trust in his provision so much that you willingly and joyfully help others.

God, help me see the blessings I have as opportunities to share with others.

Guaranteed Faithfulness

God is faithful; you were called by him into fellowship with his Son, Jesus Christ our Lord.

1 Corinthians 1:9 csb

Some guarantees are better than others. There are lifetime guarantees that are only good for a few years, and there are some guarantees that aren't even worth the paper they are written on. The guarantee is only as good as the person or company backing it.

The guarantee given in today's Scripture is one that is worth more than any gold or silver could buy. The promise of God's faithfulness and fellowship is reliable. His Word is trustworthy, and you can bet your life on it. Everything he says is true, and he will keep all of his promises.

Thank you, God, for keeping your promises. Thank you for being faithful and true to what you say.

Nothing Is Hidden

"Even before they call, I will answer;
while they are still speaking, I will hear."
ISAIAH 65:24 CSB

God doesn't ask us to call on him because he needs an update. He's not waiting for us to fill him in, and he's not in the dark about the details of our lives. He sees each day, moment, thought, and situation. He is fully aware of what is going on long before we bring it to him.

God knows you. There is nothing about you that is hidden from him. He longs for you to share your life with him, and he wants you to know that he is listening whenever you call.

God, thank you for knowing the depths of my heart. Thank you for being so attentive and kind.

God is a capable and committed defender.

Fully Equipped

God gave us a spirit not of fear but of power and love and self-control.

2 Timothy 1:7 ESV

We do not have to be slaves to fear. We don't have to let our anxieties dictate our decisions or attitudes. The Holy Spirit within us gives us power, love, and self-control. Fear will not rule us if we readily acknowledge God's Spirit.

God lives inside you and has equipped you with the tools you need. You might feel stuck in a pattern of thinking, but you are not helpless. Cling to the truth, and trust in God's transformative power.

God, thank you for the gift of the Spirit. When fear rises within me, remind me that I am strong because of you.

Unlimited Access

Let us approach the throne of grace with boldness, so that we may receive mercy and find grace to help us in time of need.

Hebrews 4:16 csb

We have been given direct access to God. We get to walk in confidently and approach the throne of grace with boldness. We don't have to be afraid that we don't belong. Through Christ, we have been invited into God's presence.

Jesus' blood has given you the ability to approach God. His perfection allows you to have eternal life despite your imperfection. He laid his life down for you so that you might experience God's grace and mercy when you need it most.

Jesus, may I stand before the Father in awe, knowing that I belong there because of what you have done.

Never Consumed

"He will wipe every tear from their eyes, and there will be no more death or sorrow or crying or pain. All these things are gone forever."

REVELATION 21:4 NLT

There is no pain that will last forever. There is no grief that will completely consume us. There is no trial that we will not overcome. Everything we experience now will one day pass away, and we will see God in his glory.

Look forward with hope because God's promise of perfection will be fulfilled. Look forward with hope because your current circumstances are not the end of the story. Look forward with hope because the best is yet to come.

God, fill me with hope for what's to come. Thank you for the promise of eternal perfection.

God Is Near

The Lord is near to all who call on him,
to all who call on him in truth.

Psalm 145:18 NIV

God is never far off. He is closer than we can understand, and he is eager to respond. Any perceived distance between us and God comes from our own perspective. He is always available, and he is always listening.

You can be as close to God as you want to be. Scripture is filled with reassurance that he is near to those who call on him, and you aren't the exception. Search for his presence, and you will find it.

God, help me to see how near you are to me. I want to feel your presence and know that you are here when I call on you.

Worth It All

May the God of hope fill you with all joy and peace as you believe so that you may overflow with hope by the power of the Holy Spirit.

ROMANS 15:13 CSB

We do not have a false sense of hope, joy, or peace. We don't manufacture them on our own, and they don't come from sources that are fleeting. Our hope, joy, and peace come directly from God, and they are eternal.

Follow God and fill your heart with truth. Devote your life to him, and he will give you hope. Offer him everything you have, and he will give you purpose. He will keep your steps steady. Life with him is worth it all.

God, fill me with hope, joy, and peace. You are worth everything I have.

God promises to finish the work he began in your life.

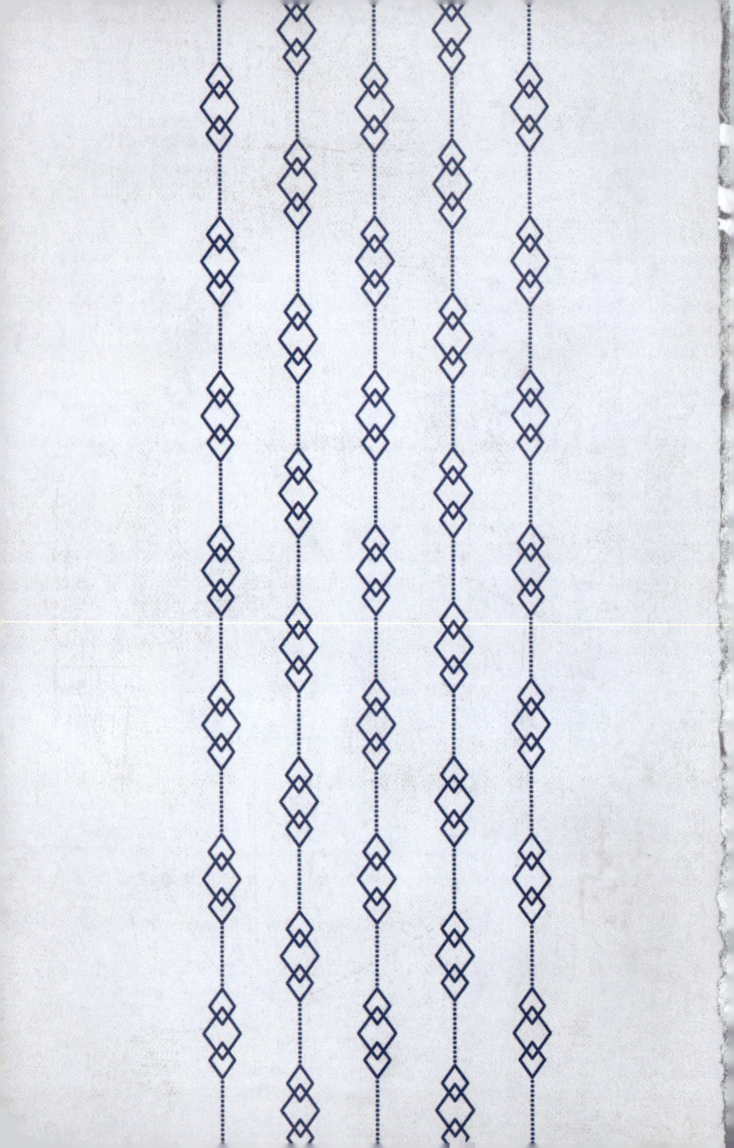

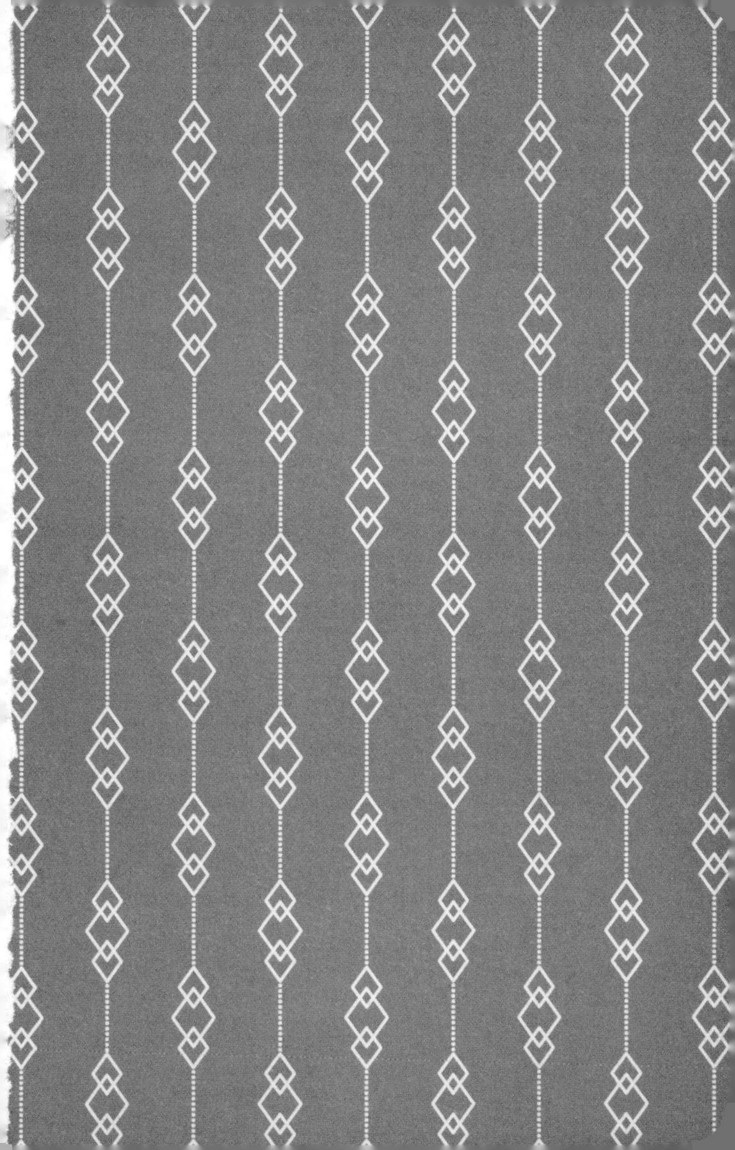